officeZen

Also by Emma Silverman

The Joy of Yoga

Yoga Twists & Turns

officeZen

101 Ways to Make Your Work Space
Calm, Happy, and Productive

Emma Silverman

Helios
press

Helios Press books may be purchased in bulk at special discounts for sales promotion, corporate gifts, fund-raising, or educational purposes. Special editions can also be created to specifications. For details, contact the Special Sales Department, Helios Press, Skyhorse Publishing, 307 West 36th Street, 11th Floor, New York, NY 10018 or info@skyhorsepublishing.com.

Helios® and Helios Press® are registered trademarks of Skyhorse Publishing, Inc.®, a Delaware corporation.

Visit our website at www.skyhorsepublishing.com.

10 9 8 7 6 5 4 3 2 1

Library of Congress Cataloging-in-Publication Data is available on file.

Cover design by Jane Sheppard
Cover photo credit: iStock

Print ISBN: 978-1-5107-1664-3
Ebook ISBN: 978-1-5107-1665-0

Printed in China

For Sara Maria Giffin

Contents

Introduction

You do not need to climb to the top of the coldest, highest mountain to be Zen. You do not need to crawl on your hands and knees, seal yourself away in a cave, or stop eating birthday cake. Most importantly, at least for these pages, you do not have to quit your job to be Zen. In *Office Zen: 101 Ways to Make Your Work Space Calm, Happy, and Productive*, you will learn how Zen can exist in any moment and any place, especially the office.

This book is divided into chapters that touch on every aspect of our work experience. From the food we eat to the relationships we create, Zen invites us to pay more attention to every part of our office life. If one aspect of your workday is feeling out of balance, simply turn to that chapter and read through quick and simple tips that will immediately change your day for the better.

These teachings can help us be present, cultivate simplicity and ease, and feel peaceful toward ourselves and others. Most of us spend more time in the office than anywhere else. It's time that you brought intention and awareness to the desk, more joy to your job, and Zen into your office!

Before Work

Preparing for the Day

1

Setting Your Alarm

Beginnings are important—and so is the beginning of each day.

Everyone knows there's a big psychological difference between waking up with an alarm and waking up whenever you please, but there's also a physiological difference, a change in how our bodies respond. Start your day off right by using an app or an alarm clock that tracks the stages of your sleep cycle. By nudging you awake when you're in the REM (Rapid Eye Movement) stage—the stage of sleep when your brain frequency most resembles the awake brain—these alarms make it easier to get out of bed and let your body adjust faster to being awake.

2
Breakfast

Breakfast is the most important meal of the day, right? Maybe not.

That oft-quoted line first came to us courtesy of an article published in 1917 in *Good Health* (a magazine edited by one Dr. Kellogg—name sound familiar?). In the century since its publication, dozens of scientific studies have been published on the subject. The conclusion? Well, it seems even the scientific community is still debating that one. If you can't think clearly without eating something first thing in the morning, eat something—preferably low in sugar and high in protein. If you're not hungry until noon, don't force yourself to eat. Nobody likes hangry office mates, but it's also a challenge to be productive while in a food coma.

3

Tea Ceremony

A traditional Japanese tea ceremony with origins in Zen Buddhism, sometimes called the Way of the Tea, can last up to four hours.

Take time at the start of every day to drink your favorite morning beverage. Let's be clear: I am not recommending setting your alarm a few hours early. Instead, pick a favorite morning beverage: Moroccan mint, strawberry-banana smoothie, orange pekoe tea, coffee so strong it can take the varnish off your floor. While preparing your favorite morning beverage, do nothing else. No radio, no morning news in the background, no discussions about money and time management with your partner. Finally, while drinking your favorite morning beverage, also do nothing. You can multitask like a champion while it's cooling down (it's okay to take baby steps on the path to Zen), but while you're drinking it, close your eyes and notice how it tastes. This whole process should take five to ten minutes, max, but it will change the spirit of your entire day.

4
Dressing the Part

I'm writing this sentence while wearing yoga pants and a thermal long-sleeved shirt that I stole from my mother. I might have a cat on my lap, cheering me on. Am I comfy? Sure. Am I writing well? You can debate that. What I definitely notice is that while wearing my pajamas, I'm more likely to take cat-petting breaks, snack breaks, chore breaks, break for the sake of breaks—you get the idea.

When I dress like a boss, I work like a boss. Studies at Northwestern and Columbia University support what you might already sense: when you wear clothing that you associate with being smart, powerful, and focused, your behavior and productivity modify accordingly.

What article of clothing makes you feel Zen? Is it a clunky plastic necklace you got at a garage sale? Own it. Is it a tie with pictures of puppies on it? I also love puppies. Is it a Christmas sweater? Make sure it's the right season, and, if so, rock it.

I know a lot of workplaces have dress codes, but you are still a uniquely fashionable being. Wear something that makes you feel good in your body so that brilliant mind of yours can do its thing.

5

The Importance of Shoes

How many of us have had nights or even *whole days* ruined because of a bad choice of footwear? I know I'm not the only one.

The state of our feet affects the health of our entire body. The health of our body helps create equanimity in our minds. Do not underestimate how important it is to wear shoes that are comfortable and fit well. It's not sexy, it's not some fancy new concept, but shoes are the most important pieces of clothing on our body. Have style, but also have arch support.

6

Your Commute

I, for one, am ready for self-driving cars. The great majority of North Americans commute to work by driving alone amid the constant threat of traffic and terrible drivers. Self-driving cars will reduce congestion, decrease the risk of accidents, increase our ability to fumble with the radio, and cut the length of most of our commutes. Until that glorious, Jetsons-like day comes, here are three out-of-the-box suggestions to add some joy to your commute:

1. I am a podcast addict. By listening to podcasts and then repeating facts I have learned from them at dinner parties, I sound much smarter than I am. Anytime you're *not already on the road*, download them, put them in listening order, and get rid of the ones where you feel the need to fast forward through the commercials.
2. Come up with intricate plot details for a film or television show. Create a family tree for the novel in your head. Design your dream home. Use these moments to yourself for creativity!
3. Happy song playlists: sing along loudly and clearly. It's good for you mentally and physically.

And for those of you who commute using public transportation? Read a great book. Take a nap. Do a crossword. Flirt with those who are receptive. You got this.

7

Running Late

We all run late. It happens. Life happens.

But even if you're running late in the car or on public transit, do you feel your pulse quicken and heart rate rise?

The next time you find yourself rushing to work, see if you can calm down the part of your brain that is also rushing. As you're sitting in the subway car and the conductor announces that it's delayed because of "garblesmark two hours xmhshsh," can your thoughts remain clear? When you're stuck at the world's longest red light, which you feel was invented just for you at this ill-timed moment, find the position of the sun in the sky.

Be in the moment, however late is it.

8

Rituals and Routines

Close your eyes and imagine a Zen Morning. What does it look like? What are you doing? What is the world outside your window doing? Focus on the details: the color of the light, the objects surrounding you, and how you are sitting.

Twenty bucks says you're not hunched into a strange position in front of your computer with a giant mug of black coffee (it's only black because you forgot to buy the milk), a child running loose somewhere in your periphery, and your partner shouting good-bye from another room.

Maybe a Zen Morning is drinking a cup of warm lemon water outside or taking five minutes to lie next to your toddler while they sleep. "Peace and quiet" is not one size fits all. Figure out what works for you—and then start doing it.

Of all the suggestions in this chapter, this one is the hardest to implement. But it's feasible. Take it one moment at a time, don't be discouraged, and start your day the way you imagine it can be.

Creating Your Work Space

Ergonomics, Cleanliness, and Feng Shui

9

Arranging Your Desk

In tenth grade, my high school social studies teacher told me, "Brevity is the key to successful communication." Similarly, simplicity is the key to Zen. How can brevity be expressed in the desk space? You can read this chapter to find out, but here are five first steps:

1. Find room for a plant on your desk. I suggest placing it in the back left corner, or at least away from wildly gesticulating hands.
2. Organize your stuff—use your drawers effectively, not as a "see no evil, hear no evil" place to put stuff you're not sure what to do with.
3. Hang or frame only one or two pictures. Your desk isn't your Facebook news feed.
4. Get rid of the clutter—file the papers or throw them out.
5. Try not to eat at your desk. If you do, makes sure to clean the container and pack it away when you're done with your food or drink.

10

Plants and Flowers

According to the principles of Feng Shui (which, strictly speaking, are separate from the practice of Zen, although there are some overlaps), placing plants and flowers strategically around your desk might help bring a little extra love or money into your life. The back right corner of your desk is the Romantic Relationships and Love section. Place a freshly cut flower, if you're looking for love, or a picture of your sweetie if you have one in this spot. The back left corner of your desk is devoted to money matters, so a vibrant green plant not only boosts your oxygen intake, but might also boost your cash flow.

11
Organization-ness Is Next to Productivity-ness

Albert Einstein is famously quoted as saying, "If a cluttered desk is a sign of a cluttered mind, of what, then, is an empty desk a sign?" It's nice to know even Einstein was wrong about something. Clean your desk. Create an organizational system. A clear, focused mind is a good thing, not something to be avoided.

12

Photographs

I've already addressed where a picture of your sweetie can go (hint: back right corner). To remind you of your support network, whoever they are, you can also add a picture to the center-left of your desk. Following Feng Shui, I recommend a recently taken photo placed in a wooden frame. This is the Family and Community area of your desk, and a photo here may help bring positive energy to this part of your life for the long term as well as the day-to-day.

13

Clearing Out the Inbox

Cubicle used to be a fancy name for "paper storage space." The electronic inbox has changed that for the modern office dweller. I know at least a few people are reading this and thinking, "Electronic inbox? Is there any other kind?" Yes, my friend born in the 1990s.

Paper or electronic, create an organizational system for your inbox and stick to it. It should feel low-stress and easy to manage. If it doesn't, it's worth taking the time to reorganize and archive anything that is no longer relevant.

14

Simplifying Your Desktop

Go to your computer's desktop. How many files and folders are hanging out there? Under five? Ten to fifteen? More than that?

Although you might argue that it makes perfect sense to you, and you know exactly where everything is, a cluttered environment takes its toll. Every time you have to pick something out of that messy desktop, the eye takes in the whole scope of what's there and so does your brain. A cleaner, streamlined desktop is more calming to the nerves. Think: folders and—shocker!—an easy-to-follow organizational system.

15

When Was the Last Time You Dusted?

I'm guessing it's no one's responsibility but your own to clean your work space and its dust, water stains, and food residues. Cleanliness lies at the heart of the Zen practice. Clean your space and feel better.

16

You Are Where You Sit

Most desk jockeys spend around eight hours a day in the same chair, at the same desk, looking at the same monitor at the same height.

This sameness causes rigidity in the neck and shoulders, back pain, insomnia, wrist issues, and a host of other problems you might already know about because you've lived through it.

This isn't a book on ergonomics—it is, however, about how the state of the body and mind are inextricably linked. If the business or organization you work at is large enough, there might be an ergonomics specialist on staff. If not, ask your employer to bring one in for the day to evaluate your work space—tell them it will reduce their health insurance premiums. If none of these options are available, take the time to do some research on your own. Your body will thank you for it.

17
Standing Desks

The jury is still out on the long-term benefits of standing desks. There is consensus, however, that variety is key. Doing any one thing for hours at a time without variation, be it standing or sitting, isn't good for the body or brain.

Until more studies are completed, I recommend doing work-related tasks standing whenever possible and sitting for the remainder of the time (flip this if you're already accustomed to standing desks). For example, stand up during phone calls, even if they're only a couple minutes long. If you're organizing paperwork, you can probably do this standing up, as well. Remember to take frequent breaks, too, and you're on your way to postural Zen!

18

The Thermostat

Does your office feel freezing cold, even in the middle of the summer?

Well, if you're a woman working in a large office setting, you're probably not alone. According to a study published in 2015 in the journal *Nature Climate Change*, the thermostats in most office buildings are set according to an antiquated formula based on the metabolic rates and clothing habits of men. For example, while the men in your office might be perfectly comfortable in their suits, women wearing dresses and skirts are turning blue in the air-conditioning.

Ladies: using your energy to stay warm takes energy away from your mental focus. Until the world catches up with the modern office, load up on sweaters and lap blankets. As my mom always says, "wear layers." Being more comfortable will make it easier for you to be Zen.

19

Lighting the Room

Ergonomics specialists, in addition to figuring out your desk and chair setup, can also help create optimal lighting for your office space to reduce eye fatigue and headaches. Create a balance between enough lighting to see without strain but not so much that you're squinting against glare. Also take into consideration the color of the lightbulbs or fluorescent lights used by your office. Ideally, natural sunlight is a part of this plan. If you're in a cube that never sees the light of day, turn the page for some alternatives.

20

Happy Lights

How much natural sunlight we receive and our mood are directly correlated. Bright light exposure raises our serotonin levels, a hormone that contributes to our feelings of happiness. While it isn't the cheapest solution, light therapy lamps are great options for those stuck in offices for almost every hour of daylight—a likely scenario if you live away from the equator.

Some forward-thinking insurance companies cover all or part of the cost of light therapy lamps. If you experience Seasonal Affective Disorder (SAD) or other mental health issues related to a lack of daylight, see if this is an option for you.

21

Windows

Logically, you might think that if your office is blessed with a window, you should face your desk toward it. Energetically, you're creating a Feng Shui FOMO: directing all of your energy toward the outside world instead of your work while simultaneously turning your back on the rest of your office. This is especially problematic if you have a position of authority and want to be approachable.

Face your desk toward the door and allow the sunshine to come in from the window and shine a light on your work.

22
Sage, Crystals, and Other New-Age Gizmos

I'm married to a scientist who doesn't let me get away with talking about what it means to be an Aries, what chakras are open or closed, or whether the energy of our apartment feels stagnant (sorry, Feng Shui practitioners).

If placing a crystal by your door frame makes you feel better, do it. If "smudging" sage at home at the end of the workday helps you transition, sage away. If reading your coworkers' horoscopes helps you be more compassionate toward them and the struggles they're facing, I know a few great websites.

We don't know if these "new age" things work or are true—only you know if they work for you.

Sharing the Space

Bosses, Coworkers, and Work Relationships

23

Dating in the Workplace

I have, on occasion, dated yoga students of mine. It's not something I'm shout-from-the-rooftops proud of, but it has happened. When things ended—and they all ended—they stopped coming to my classes, and I was left hoping they found a different class that worked for them rather than giving up the practice entirely. On the other hand, I have friends who met and fell in love in the workplace (and sometimes your workplace happens to be a yoga studio or a meditation center) and they have fond memories of the experience.

If it's not against office policy, I think it's fine to date in the workplace. From experience, though, I recommend sitting down at the beginning of the relationship (whether it consists of hookups when you're bored of watching Netflix alone or a path to growing old together) and discussing office etiquette and exit plans. Specifically, how are we going to behave at work together? How are we going to behave at work together if things don't work out? Do that, and make sure those around you feel comfortable, and even if it isn't for forever, things should be okay.

24

Bring Your Pet to Work Day

Since June 24, 1999, the United States has celebrated Take Your Dog to Work Day as an annual event. This past year, the organization that helps promote the event estimated that more than 100,000 people brought their dog (or pet) into work. While this might upset office "pawlitics" in some workplaces, especially if you have allergy-sensitive desk mates, spending time with our four-footed friends might be just the thing to keep our day Zen.

25

Office Birthdays

You don't have to eat the birthday cake, even if it's been precut, even if someone is handing it to you. Some say, "Life is short, eat the damn cake." I say, in larger offices, there are too many opportunities to eat things that make you feel terrible. Perhaps bring some mindfulness into what you're putting into your mouth. At times, eat the damn cake.

26

Office Clubs and Organizations

Social groups around the office are a great way to integrate into your community, especially if you've relocated to a new city for work. I know someone who didn't get the office dynamics at her new job until she joined their kickball league.

Just make sure you do the things you like; if you're someone who shivered at the mere mention of the word *kickball*, find the office mates who want to hear about your Top Ten Books of the Year or your recipe for vegan cheesecake. I know I would!

27

Office Culture

Pretend that you're in a room with your oldest, closest friend. Describe to her the culture of your office. Is it hyper-social? Opportunistic? Laid-back? Tech-y? Now, imagine her response. Would she say your personality aligns with the culture of the place where you spend more waking hours than anywhere else in the world?

If you catch yourself saying you hate everyone you work with ("they're all idiots" is a phrase I have both heard and said before), maybe it's the culture and not the individuals.

If you can move to a new organization or business, or even a different unit in your current workplace, try to find an office culture that more obviously aligns with your own. Ask questions about this during your job interview and head to the Internet to do research. If changing jobs isn't an option for you (I know it isn't always that easy to just pick up and leave), perhaps the ability to step back and see clearly where the misalignment occurs can help create a sense of control over your situation.

28

Drinking with Coworkers

The stereotype of the drunken holiday party is already overdone; you know what that looks like in the movies and in real life and everyone knows how it ends (spoiler alert: not well). Zen teaches us to notice when we're running away from the things in our life that are difficult to face. Only you know your impulse behind these social gatherings, so decide whether they're bringing the cheer of your social life to your workplace or the dreariness of your workplace to your social life.

29

Girl Scout Cookies
and Other Donations

I once worked in an office comprising almost entirely women in their late twenties to early forties. It wasn't uncommon to get hit up at least a couple times a month: for a wedding card and present, for some kid's cookie fund-raiser, or for a baby-shower fund. At one point, I realized I had to start budgeting for these requests.

If you truly want to give to all of these occasions (and have the cash on hand to support your generous spirit), there's no reason not to. Doing so and complaining about it later, however, will not give you any karma points.

To stop these requests from coming your way, talk to the party planner in private (I imagine it's usually the same person making the rounds). Don't lie or come up with excuses, but let her know directly and Zen-ly why you can't, or won't, contribute this time around. As we've seen in other chapters, you're not responsible for her reaction, only how you communicate your needs.

30

Mediators and Conflict Management

Mediators are trained, impartial professionals who step in when two parties are unwavering in their disagreement and cannot, on their own, come to a peaceable conclusion. I've used one when my landlord wanted to keep my entire security deposit because I burned a pencil eraser–sized hole into a kitchen countertop (hot pan, short story). I often wish one was handy during extended family visits.

If you ever were in the middle of a conflict and wanted to shout, "Is anyone else hearing this? Doesn't this *other person* sound absolutely crazy?" a mediator is the person you could say that to. Preferably with no shouting.

Mediators can come from your HR department, which might have someone on staff or will hire someone from a mediation service on a temporary basis. One of the basic tenets of mediation is that it stays confidential, so you can speak freely and honestly. If one of the most challenging aspects of your office life is continual struggles with an individual, mediation can help solve it.

31

Asking for a Raise the Zen Way

The best way to ask for a raise is to ask when you have earned it, not when you need it. Instead of making the "ask" about money or politics, show your commitment to the organization and to your tasks, and use positive, thoughtful language. Make a list of talking points and stick to them. Ask fearlessly and listen without emotional attachment to how your supervisor responds.

32

R.E.S.P.E.C.T.

Everyone you meet and interact with is in some ways a reflection of yourself. In this way, we keep meeting ourselves again and again. With each interaction, we have the opportunity for a different outcome.

Recognize the continuity of experience between yourself and your peers, bosses, and those you lead—not the separation. Zen teaches us that in meditation and in daily life we must seek answers in the space of the heart. Teach respect by example, respecting yourself and others around you.

33

Conscious Communication

During my yoga teacher training, a part of our curriculum was Conscious Communication. I had two personal takeaways from this training that have informed every disagreement I've had since then.

The first lesson I learned was to frame discussions around actions. This can be summarized as: "When you do this, I feel . . ." In this way, we don't presuppose how others are feeling or their intent. We only speak to what we know: what they did and how we felt about it.

The second, and perhaps the more important, is to truly listen. Let people finish their sentences. Allow for a few moments of silence after they speak to respond internally to what they said. Finally, reply first with what you heard them say, or how you interpreted what they said, before moving on to your opinion or the next topic.

Conscious Communication is contagious. Start a trend and change the office dialogue.

34

Negative Languaging

Notice if you or others around you are using negative language. This is especially harmful if the naysayer in question is very generous with exactly what's wrong with a project proposal, layout, or presentation, but suspiciously quiet about what's working and ways to make it even better.

If you, or your peers, are consistently using negative language when discussing work, use your super-strong Zen mindfulness to be aware of it as it's happening. Instead of calling coworkers out on it, you can restate what they said (using Conscious Communication) but use positive words instead of negative.

Here's an example:

Less-than-Zen coworker: "The font on these slides is ridiculous. No one will be able to read Helvetica in 10-point from the back of the room!"

Super-Zen you: "I hear you saying that the slides would look great with a clear font in a larger, easy-to-read size?"

Positive Languaging is also contagious (just like Conscious Communication). Before you know it, things will be a lot better.

35

Fragrances/Perfumes

Most of the yoga studios I attend and where I work have guidelines for the students that request no strong fragrances or perfumes. Because of allergies and personal preference (not everyone loves patchouli, shockingly), some offices are setting similar guidelines. Be conscious of your B.O., whatever the scent may be, and talk to HR if someone else's scent is making you sneeze.

If you love the smell of perfume, consider bringing some natural perfume into your space with some fresh flowers—they'll provide beauty as well as a scent to make you smile!

36

Volunteering Outside
the Office

It is mighty Zen indeed to act for the sake of action and without expectation of reward.

I spent a year volunteering with AmeriCorps, a program of the US federal government that matches adults with public service activities (you are provided with a small stipend and an education award after completing a year of service). That experience forever altered how I view my time, labor, and worth—for the better.

Volunteering as a community activity is a great way to build connections and strengthen bonds with your coworkers. The organization where you work might even be willing to sponsor your activities by donating money, providing tools and resources, or even giving you days off to volunteer.

Give it a try. As they say, the life you change the most might be your own.

37

Gossip

There is a quote attributed to the Zen master Ummon Zenji: "Men of unmeasurable greatness are tossed about in the ebb and flow of words." This is a *koan,* or a Zen parable, which is intended give the recipient something to meditate on without providing an easy answer. If Ummon Zenji had sat himself in the middle of your modern office space, would he have observed anyone getting tossed about? Did they do something to deserve it? Even if so, in which ways are they great?

38

Energetic Black Holes

I refer to some people as Energetic Black Holes. No matter how much time and energy you give to these people, it feels like it's never reciprocated. After these interactions, you feel exhausted, like they just sucked the life out of you.

Have compassion for Energetic Black Holes; it's likely their lives are challenging and they need to rely on others for energy and happiness as opposed to finding it in themselves. At the same time, identify these people in your life and, when you spend time with them, be incredibly aware of your own energy levels and back off as needed.

39

Working While Female

The whole non-attachment, selfless, and gentle thing can be really, really hard when you're a kick-ass business lady-star and not being acknowledged for your genius. As of June 2016, women held only 21 out of the 500 CEO positions on the S&P 500. I struggle with finding the Zen in this situation—I'm angry about this disparity, but know that my anger isn't creating change.

The Tao Te Ching says that in action, timing is everything. It also says not to start fights and not to blame. If you're caught working while female and coming up short, don't sit by idly, gritting your teeth and trying to practice detachment. Do something about it, but in doing so, remember the principles of honest communication and respect.

Working from Home

Creating a Home Office

40
Organizing Your Home Office

These days, after years working in an office setting, I work primarily from home. I'm not the only one spending time tapping the keyboard in my living room: a 2015 Gallup poll estimates that 37 percent of US workers currently telecommute or have done so in the past.

You can follow many of the same guidelines for setting up your work space at home as setting up your desk at the office. Some special considerations for the home office will be addressed throughout the rest of this chapter.

41

Setting Work Hours

If you're working for yourself, there's no right or wrong time to work. You just have to get the work done—whether that's wrapping things up at 3:00 a.m. or starting the workday at noon. That's it: no judgment, and no worries.

It gets a bit more complicated if you rely on exchanging information with others while you work. My friend Ethan lived in India for over a year while working for a software company in New York. He ended up keeping some pretty strange hours to communicate with his coworkers.

I recommend maintaining the schedule closest to what you would naturally follow. If that doesn't align with the schedule of the people you connect with, set aside an hour or two outside of that schedule for emails and conference calls. Let your coworkers know the plan so you can use that time effectively and efficiently.

42

What's My Motivation Here?

Zen can really help you here. Just like working the muscles in your body, when you give the mind exercises to calm down and focus, it will get stronger over time. Having a meditation practice, then, strengthens our ability to get motivated.

So work that mind muscle—and inspiration will follow!

43

On Not Doing the Dishes, and Other Household Chores

Before I can get any work done from home, I need to clean everything. I cannot write from my kitchen table if the remnants of my better half's avocado toast is sitting in front of me. This is both a great motivator for keeping a tidy house and a great distraction technique for getting zero work done.

Cleanliness and organization are good things, but not at the expense of the time you set aside to work. If you're like me, make sure the house is work-ready before you plan on clocking in, and don't start cleaning when you would otherwise be doing your job.

44

Taking Breaks

Check out "Stepping Away for a Moment" on page 101 to find out the recommended work versus break-time ratio. If you work from home, there's the added bonus that your work "breaks" can also be super productive. Yesterday, my brain break involved walking across the street to buy a loaf of bread and then returning back to my desk. Other times, when I'm feeling a little fried, I take ten minutes to check the mail or fold the laundry.

At the end of your work day, you might find that not only has the work gotten done (and with increased productivity and fewer mistakes), but all your errands are done, too.

45

A Separate Space

If you can afford it, set up a separate room for your office. Every room in a house has a primary purpose and when we're in that room, we will naturally gravitate toward that objective.

Most of us, myself included, don't have the luxury of a home office. If you find yourself continually distracted by your home and its needs (cleaning, food replacement, cat petting), create a place outside the home where you habitually work. If you need suggestions, a few of them are on the next page. By visiting location, you are sending a message to your brain that it's go time, and your productivity will respond accordingly.

46

Coffee Shops, etc.

Here's a list of places you can work to get yourself out of the house, but that don't require a caffeine intake:

- City libraries
- Friends' houses
- Coworking spaces
- Rent-a-desk apps (Airbnb has one)
- Public libraries
- Bars
- Bookstores
- Parks (many city parks in North America now have Wi-Fi)
- Bakeries
- Diners
- Hotel lobbies
- Anywhere else with free Wi-Fi

47
Taking Vacations (Real Ones)

Because I am self-employed, I find it hard to take vacations. No one is giving me vacation days, so every day I don't work is a day I'm not getting paid. It's an unhealthy mindset that I'm trying to kick.

The Tao Te Ching speaks about the importance of emptying our minds to find peace. We need a break every once and awhile to stay healthy, sane, and Zen. I recommend budgeting at least ten days of vacation time into your schedule each year—and committing to take the time off.

48

Social Media

Does your job require you to use social media? If so, congratulations. You, my friend, get paid to do what most of us do for free.

For the rest of us, it's important to notice not only how many hours a day we're logging into our preferred methods of social media, but how often we check it. Giving yourself a "hooray you finished one page of the presentation" Facebook check-in isn't really the best kind of motivator. And social media breaks aren't the kind of breaks I was talking about in other chapters—the point is to step *away* from your computer, not just to a new tab.

If you have an addiction to social media (and, yes, addiction—there are support groups), figure out some method to keep track of the frequency and duration of your log-ins. Create a reasonable limit and stick to it.

49

Work Groups

Yardenne is one of my best friends. When we started our work dates, though, we barely knew each other. I just knew that we were both writers and that I was terrible at self-motivation. We set up a weekly meet up at our local food co-op and would bring our notebooks and laptops.

We never, ever got any work done.

I am entirely to blame for this. She is a brilliant writer and translator and knows how to get things done. Turns out, I was just looking for someone to procrastinate with.

The moral of this story? Work groups are great, if they're devoid of people like me. If you truly need motivation and are tired of asking your cats for feedback, find an already successful work group and ask if you can join. If that's not an option, start one of your own and fill it with people who really know how to pound the keyboard in a convincing fashion.

You'll find success—just don't invite me.

50

Valuing Your Time

When you begin a new enterprise, it can be hard to figure out how to value your time. Do your research: ask others in a similar field (but not your competition, that's just awkward), poke around on the Internet, and—if your field required an advanced degree or training—ask the people who taught you what the expected salary should be.

People will ask you for discounts and freebies. Don't reply immediately if they do; give yourself enough time to consider their request and how to respond. If it's a real low-ball, prepare a response that kindly and firmly clarifies your worth. If it's a fair request, for example, they're seeking your expertise on an ongoing basis or for a larger contract, then run the numbers to estimate realistically how much time is required for the project and what your hourly rate will work out to be. Learn how to feel comfortable talking about money.

The bottom line: if you've invested in yourself and your expertise, then others need to be ready to invest in you, too.

On the Road Again

Traveling for Work

51
Jet Lag

Here are a few tips to help combat jet lag:

1. Drink a ton of water on the plane. Don't feel guilty about making everyone get up so you can use the bathroom; in fact, getting up and moving around every once and awhile is also good for you.
2. Even if you're exhausted upon arrival, don't nap for more than twenty minutes (set an alarm). Go to sleep according to the new time zone.
3. Light therapy. I talk about this in the Creating Your Work Space chapter, beginning on page 11. Talk to a doctor about timing your light therapy to adjust your circadian rhythm to your new location.
4. Melatonin. It's a "natural remedy," but you still would want to check in with your doctor before taking any pill on a semi-regular basis.
5. Coffee. Never fails, right?

52
A Meditation for Work Trips

Here's a meditation routine to help fight the fatigue that can come with long work trips. It focuses on creating a sense of grounding in the physical body when everything else is in flux:

Close your eyes and bring your awareness to your hands. Notice any sensation in your hands, notice the temperature of your hands and the feeling of air passing over your hands. Now narrow your focus to your right thumb. Can you go through the same process of noticing, but just with awareness of your right thumb? Repeat the same for each of your fingers. If it gets more challenging, meet that challenge with equanimity and without judgment.

Repeat this action for your feet. First notice both feet and then narrow your awareness, repeating the process for each toe. It can be pretty difficult, but relax your mind and give it a try!

53

Repeat Destinations

While I was living in Madison, Wisconsin, and working in software, I was assigned a client in Philadelphia. At least a couple times a month, I had to fly to Philly and spend the work week there, staying in the Marriott across from City Hall. This lasted over a year. In that time, I made a life for myself in Philly. I met up with friends from college, planned visits with family who lived nearby, and joined the University of Pennsylvania's Tae Kwon Do team.

It can suck to travel for work. I know at times it felt like I was missing my life. But if it's your job to travel, don't stop living life when you're on the road. Integrate it in, and make your life even fuller.

54

New Horizons

For every new place you have to travel for work, make a promise to yourself—right now—that you will see something, taste something, smell something, *experience* something totally new. Even if you're only there for a day and especially if you feel like you're so busy you don't have enough time.

Take a picture of your new thing. Post it to Instagram. Get some followers. Start a revolution.

55

Friends and Family in Distant Cities

If you're lonely on the road, turn to social media. People move around constantly, and even if you're totally positive you don't know anyone in Dubai, Dubuque, or Dublin, you might be pleasantly surprised. Even if you don't know the person first-hand, your college roommate's cousin might live in town and be happy to show you around in exchange for a pint of beer. You might not be BFFs forever, but having someone to talk to outside of your colleagues can do wonders for your mental health.

56

Food To-Go

My favorite part of traveling for work was the food (although, to be honest, my favorite part of almost any event is the food). On work trips, I discovered Ethiopian food, got asked out on a date in an Indian buffet, and, most importantly, learned how to eat in a restaurant alone.

Follow the same meal guidelines as in your office space (simple, healthy, and in moderation), but don't be afraid to go outside of your comfort zone and try new things.

57

OM in the Airport

It's very *en vogue* to have a yoga or meditation space in the airport. Here's a list of airports that (as of writing this page) have a space to find some Zen:

- Albany, NY
- Albuquerque
- Amsterdam-Schipol
- Burlington
- Chicago-O'Hare
- Chicago-Midway
- Detroit
- Frankfurt
- Helsinki
- Hong Kong
- Hyderabad
- London-Heathrow
- London-Gatwick
- New York–JFK
- Raleigh-Durham
- San Diego
- San Francisco
- Singapore-Changi
- Sioux Falls
- Vancouver

If you need a space to meditate and the airport you're traveling through isn't listed above, non-denominational chapels are available in most major airports and provide a space for quiet contemplation.

Stimulate Your Senses

Maintaining Focus and Sanity

58

Colors to Inspire Creativity

A study from Miami University in Ohio, published in 1999, found that the color white, which it seems most offices are painted, is linked to headaches, feelings of nausea, irritability, and eye fatigue. You might not be able to repaint your office, but you can add some color to liven up the space—and your mind! Here are some examples:

- Can't be creative because you're too stressed out to think? Put up a wall hanging or picture that features calming blues and light greens—think nature colors, like aqua, teal, and pine.
- Feeling a major energy slump? Wear a fire-red scarf into the office today.
- Midweek blahs? Yellow is said to create cheer, so perhaps place a few sunshine-filled objects artfully around your desk. Whatever the mood, color can help spark your creativity!

59

Stress Balls and Stones

My college roommate lives in Girdwood, Alaska, outside of Anchorage. The last time I visited her, in January 2015, I found a lovely, perfectly smooth stone, which proceeded to save my life for the next five months.

The winter of 2015 turned out to be the coldest winter on record for the northeastern United States, where I lived at the time. I was stuck indoors, it was dark, and my work space had no windows. I kept that stone in the pocket of my cardigan every day and when I felt my brain starting to sizzle, I would take my thumb to the stone in concentric circles. I don't understand the science of it, I just know it worked. "Worry stones," "worry dolls," "stress balls," and the like exist in many cultures throughout the world and have for a long time. The Internet is bursting with different things you can buy to hold in your hand and feel less stressed out, but I think it's as simple as beginning with a stone.

60

Music and Melodies

While writing the proposal for this book, I started to go stir-crazy sitting alone in my apartment. I went to the nearest, hippest coffee shop and set up. Within five minutes, very loud (although, yes, very hip) music started playing and I spent thirty minutes trying to ignore it without actually writing anything. I ended up sitting in an unused hallway at my yoga studio, my laptop plugged into an outlet running along the floor.

Depending on the task at hand, music can either help or hurt. If you have an incredibly boring or repetitive task, music can improve your mood and your efficiency. On the other hand, if your work for the day requires intense focus or acquiring a new skill, listening to your favorite tunes will probably just distract you (as I learned the hard way).

If you use music to drown out the background noise of a chatty open office, try listening to classical music or ambient music without lyrics. Worst-case scenario if that doesn't work—there's always the hallway.

61

Quiet Spaces

Find spaces that provide quiet not just for your ears, but all of your senses. For example, a space away from the chatter of coworkers, fluorescent lights, and break-room smells. If they're constantly stimulated, our senses can become dulled and tired. Plan a discovery mission around your office space and unearth hidden spots in which you can recharge.

62

Smells to Perk You Up

Did you know that of all of our senses, smell is most connected to the brain's emotional center and can most easily trigger memories? Maybe you've experienced that for yourself, when you smell popcorn and remember your favorite movie theater or get a whiff of a pine-scented candle and have a flashback to hikes in the forest.

Scents can also benefit us at work. Here are a few that might help: rosemary (memory retention), citrus (concentration), cinnamon (also concentration and focus), and peppermint (energizing). You can make tea using one of these ingredients—even if you don't drink it, the smell alone might have the desired effect.

Just remember: If you do use scents in your personal desk space, make sure that it doesn't waft over to your office mates. What might be lovely for you may not have the same effect if it overpowers everyone else.

63

Snacks that Boost Energy

Technically speaking, the calories we associate mostly with food are a measure of all forms of energy, so any food going into your digestive system will provide an energy boost. What we're looking for, then, is a delightful snack that provides energy without a crash an hour or two after eating.

Kevin Klatt, a doctoral candidate in Nutritional Sciences at Cornell University (and—full disclosure—a friend), told me: "I recommend pairing a fiber-rich carb with a protein and fat. . . . Most folks crave the carbs when they want a quick energy boost, and the protein/fat helps slow the digestion so you get a steady stream of glucose into the blood."

Kevin recommended a yummy DIY trail mix of oats, dried fruit, and the nuts/seeds combination of your choosing. Other easy snacks include dried edamame, yogurt (nonfat to 2%), and string cheese.

64

Caffeine

In the first chapter, I mentioned the Japanese tea ceremony. Let me be clear: a whole bunch of caffeine is being consumed in the green tea that's a part of those ceremonies. Zen texts do not say you shouldn't drink coffee or are a bad person for doing so. There is, however, a correlation in Zen between attachment and unhappiness. If you are super addicted to your caffeine, physically, emotionally, and spiritually, it might be time to back off a bit. Use some of the other tips in this book to boost your energy and your alertness.

65

Go Upside-down

Want something even better than coffee, in my totally and completely biased opinion? Try going upside-down!

I know in most offices there aren't a lot of options that allow you to stick your legs up into the air without looking like a crazy person. If it's possible where you work, though, the benefits are huge: improved circulation, increased blood flow to the brain, boosted immune system, and the use of gravity to send newly oxygenated blood throughout the body.

Start off by gently folding your body forward, softly bending the knees and arms hanging loosely toward the floor. This is the least crazy-looking and one of the most gentle on your body (if you have any concerns about doing an inversion, though, check in with your doctor).

If you have a yoga (or acrobatics) practice, any inversion, practiced safely and with knowledge of your body, will do the trick.

66

Shake Things Up

In Madison, Wisconsin, I lived in a housing cooperative with thirty other people. Ken, the lovely gentleman who lived directly above me, was a farmer who woke up around the time you would expect. Ken liked to start his day with a few minutes of jumping on a small, personal trampoline. Above my head.

Eventually, I discussed this with him and he explained that jumping up and down helps move lymphatic fluid (a major part of your immune system—lymph attacks bacteria like a Stark attacks a Lannister), helps get your heart rate going, and gets blood flowing through your body. Seeing as Ken made a good argument, and he was only jumping for a few minutes, I saw no point in asking him to quit.

In fact, I "jumped" on the bandwagon. When I feel myself getting sluggish, I do about twenty jumping jacks, wait for my heart rate to calm down, and then sit back down to work. It takes less than minute, but makes a huge difference.

67

How Bright Is Your Computer Screen?

This is a plug for f.lux.

F.lux is a free app that changes the color of your computer's display depending on the time of day. As they say on their website, "During the day, computer screens look good—they're designed to look like the sun. But, at 9:00 p.m., 10:00 p.m., or 3:00 a.m., you probably shouldn't be looking at the sun."

This app should help if you're experiencing insomnia that's related to using your computer late at night and might also help with eye strain.

68

Beautiful Things

Place small, attractive things in your work space that remind you of beauty. Every once and awhile, look over at them and smile.

Taking Care of Your Body

Healthy Body for a Healthy Mind

69

Are You Breathing?

Take a deep breath: inhale through your nose and exhale through your mouth. Repeat two more times (or until you're feeling better).

70

Posture

Stack your head over your heart and your heart over your hips. Keep your feet solidly planted on the floor and knees aligned with or slightly higher than your hips. Use a lumbar support if it's available and feels good. Don't cross your legs. Bring your buttocks to the back of the chair seat, but don't lean back into the chair. Maintain the natural curves of your spine. Take breaks from sitting every thirty minutes at least.

Keep breathing.

71

Yoga in the Office

In his collection of essays, *Awake in the World: Teachings from Yoga and Buddhism for Living an Engaged Life*, Michael Stone writes, "Physiology and psychology are two ends of the same stick. You can't work on one without the other." Simply put, you can't have a Zen mind without a Zen body.

Yoga in the office space is a great step toward a Zen body. It's a perk in many offices and is becoming more popular every day. Employers realize that happy, healthy employees benefit the organization as a whole.

Talk to your HR department about organizing yoga classes during the lunch hour in one of the conference rooms. Offer to push aside the tables and chairs and replace them after the class, and pitch in as an office to pay the teacher (usually it works out to just a few dollars a person per class). This is a huge step toward bringing more Zen into the workplace.

72

A Wrist Stretch to Help Prevent Carpal Tunnel Syndrome

Reach your right arm out directly in front of you, with the back of your hand parallel to the ground, palm facing up. Draw your fingers back (like an upside-down STOP hand signal). With your left hand, gently pull your pinky finger back and hold for one breath. Repeat with every finger from pinky to thumb. Repeat with your left hand extended. Afterward, roll out your wrists in both directions. Repeat once a day.

73

Shoulder Tension Release

From your seat, sit up tall and elongate your spine. On an inhale (through the nose) bring your shoulders to your ears and close your eyes. Hold the breath in for a count of five and then exhale through the mouth and simultaneously let the shoulders release. Repeat three to five times, as often as needed throughout the day, or whenever you feel the need to yell at a coworker.

74

Lower Back Stretch

Often, when our lower back feels tight, it's actually because it is *overstretched* and not tight from being inflexible. At our keyboards, we tend to sit in a perpetual forward fold, overstretching the entire back, neck, and shoulders.

For your lower back, I recommend a gentle backbend or seated twist a few times a day. Place your hands on your knees for a few rounds of seated cat/cow, moving the spine with the breath (if you're not familiar with that yoga move, do a quick Internet search). Afterward, sit up tall and twist your upper body to the right, placing both hands on the outside of your right thigh. Hold for five cycles of breath and then switch direction.

75

Reducing Eye Strain

One of the main issues with staring at a computer screen is proximity. Think of how your eyes felt during high school biology when you had to squint into a microscope. It's a lot of work, just like looking at a screen and small type just a foot from your face.

Every fifteen to twenty minutes, take a break from staring at your screen. It isn't enough just to look away, though. Reduce the strain on your eyes by staring at something in the far distance (as far as you can in your office space) for about 30 seconds, or as long as it takes you to sing the alphabet song.

76

Drink Water

Place a large container of water on your desk and within your field of vision. Use breaks to fill up your water bottle as a marvelous excuse to give your eyes a break from the computer screen. If you don't like the taste of water (yes, I know you exist), keep a slice of lemon or cucumber in your water bottle. Watch the water magically disappear throughout the day. Be healthier because of this magic trick.

77

Eat Food (But Not Too Much)

Nutrition author Michael Pollan famously wrote, "Eat food. Not too much. Mostly plants." Zen nutritionists would agree, although they might alter the last bit to "only plants." To maintain your focus during the workday, eat small, simple meals. If you find that you're still hungry later, head back to the previous chapter to plan healthy snacks to keep you going the rest of your day.

78

The Physical Response to Stress

I don't want to talk about stress in a way that will make you stressed out. I do, however, want to highlight how important it is to deal with both the instigators and the physical responses to stress as opposed to taking the "see no evil, hear no evil" response.

John Muir (the naturalist and environmental philosopher) wrote, "When we try to pick out anything by itself, we find it hitched to everything else in the Universe." When you experience psychological stress, it also affects every part of your body. It acts on all of the systems: musculosketal, respiratory, nervous, cardiovascular, gastrointesinal, immune, endocrine, and reproductive. Your body and mind are a brilliant, interconnected universe. Acknowledge and manage stress so neither has to suffer.

79

Slippers under the Desk

I wasn't introduced to the concept of slippers at work until I moved to Canada. Here, it's what all of the cool desk jockeys do. Business up top and bedtime at your feet is an unconventional look, but at least you're warm and comfy.

80

Sleeping on the Job

While all the rage in preschool, most North Americans stop taking naps once we reach primary school. We should have kept napping. Naps reduce the risk of numerous health problems, increase our cognitive performance, and even improve our overall mood.

The current recommendation is a twenty-minute nap just about when you start craving that afternoon coffee break.

Mind Matters

Meditations on Mental Health and Productivity

The Three Steps
to Seated Meditation

1. Calm the body: stop squirming, notice your desire to keep squirming.
2. Calm the breath: smooth out any erraticism in the breath, find a fluid inhale and exhale.
3. Calm the mind: bring your awareness to your thoughts, watch where the mind goes with equanimity and zero judgment.

82

Inspiring Focus

Someone once told me that people can only pay attention for as many minutes as their age. There's a reason the tips and tricks in this book are all one page long! Humans have surprisingly short attention spans, which are getting even shorter in the digital age. This affects how long we can focus on books about office Zen, our work, and even our social interactions. Ever have someone check their phone in the middle of telling them a story? Ever been that person checking their phone?

Being more engaged and focused in the workplace will help you be more attentive outside the office. Notice what keeps you on task, maybe using the Stimulate Your Senses chapter of this book (starting on page 65), or maybe by practicing something that requires focus while you're at home (for example: yoga, tai chi, learning an instrument, meditating, painting, or knitting). With increased focus, you'll be calmer and more relaxed, too.

83

Mantras (You Don't Have to Say Them Out Loud)

My mantra is: *Thank you for everything, I have no complaints whatsoever.* I say it when things are amazing and I wouldn't change anything, even if a magical genie showed up complete with a lamp and three wishes. Mostly, though, I say it when things kind of suck and I need to be reminded of the fact that they will not always suck. Nothing is permanent, which is sometimes really great and sometimes kind of scary. My mantra, which works really well for me, helps me be in the moment—whatever it looks like.

If there are words or phrases that make you smile when you hear them, say them to yourself in your head. They can be the lines to a pop song (hello, Taylor Swift and "Shake It Off"), an inspirational quote, or a line from a religious text. The only rule for your *Office Zen* mantra is this: it makes you feel good.

84

Wishing Others Good Will

There's a meditation technique called "Loving Kindness" or *"Metta"* (a Sanskrit word that can translate as "goodwill") meditation. I've modified it here to help bring some kindness to the office space:

1. Close your eyes and imagine someone you really love is around. Someone who has always helped you, always has a smile for you, and always brightens your day. In your mind, say to the image of that person: "May you be happy. May you be healthy. May you be peaceful." Repeat that phrase three times.

2. Next, imagine someone in the office who you don't really know, but perhaps would like to get to know better. They're basically a neutral figure with no major good or bad feelings associated with them. Repeat the last stage of step one, but say it to this neutral figure.

3. Next, imagine someone who regularly makes your day worse. When you have to interact with them, you get that tight feeling in your chest and queasiness in your stomach. Against your instincts, say the same phrases with the same positive energy.

4. Finally, see yourself. See yourself happy, dancing, smiling, holding and being held. Wish yourself the same blessing.

85

Feeling Overwhelmed

The first step to feeling less overwhelmed is to give yourself credit for being able to assess the situation and notice that things aren't right. Realize that the craziness of the situation does not mean that you yourself are, or have to feel, crazy. Keep that eagle-eye perspective, figure out what needs to change, and then do it. Fearlessly and compassionately.

86

Meditating on the Job

There are many different styles of meditation and no single correct definition of what meditation is. When I leave my apartment, I check to make sure I have my wallet, cell phone, and keys. Sometimes, I catch myself checking three or four times. It's not Alzheimer's, it's not paranoia. It's just that every single time I check for those items, I am doing it absentmindedly. One definition of meditation is to be present-minded instead of absentminded.

Perhaps, for you, meditating on the job is paying exquisite attention to the task at hand: if someone were to walk into your office at any given moment and ask what you had spent the last five minutes doing, you would have a complete and detailed answer (although I sincerely hope you don't have that kind of boss).

Notice what you're doing as you do it. You'll do a better job and enjoy the task at hand more. In this way, you can achieve the calmness and clarity of mind that meditation provides while working. Not to mention that, according to a University of Wisconsin MRI study, people who meditate can increase activity in the "happiness" section of the brain. Well worth it, in my opinion!

87

Visualizations

My friend Heather came up with the idea of the fanta-bummer. You know how when you fantasize about something you lie on your back in a wide, green field, close your eyes, and think of something you really want in all sorts of amazing, beautiful details?

Yeah, no one I know actually does anything remotely like that, either.

Most people I know, though, do manage to find the time to fanta-bummerize on the regular. That's when you lie in bed at night or sit rigidly in the office and think about something you really don't want in all sorts of terrifying, stressful details.

Try not to do that.

There's the saying: worrying is like praying for what you don't want. It's not easy to change the habits of our minds, but to find our small piece of Zen, we have to try.

88

Walking Meditation

Traditionally, walking meditation was used to provide a break between sessions of seated meditation. More realistically, it can provide a break between sessions of responding to email.

Begin your meditation by walking slowly, aligned with the movement of your breath. Become more aware of the shifting of weight and innate balance work that occurs as you walk. Be present with the body, but also your surroundings. The mind will wander, just as in seated meditation. Gently, without recriminations, bring your awareness back.

Take five minutes of your day to try out walking meditation. If the weather is decent, head outside. Don't worry if you're in a place where others can see you—walking meditation looks a lot like pacing, but with a completely opposite frame of mind.

89

Positive Affirmations

Positive affirmations are short sentences that we repeatedly say or think to ourselves to boost our confidence and emotional well-being. They are mantras that start with the word "I." For example, while preparing a big presentation, you might say, "I am a rock star innovator and office queen (or duke, or some other royal figure)." Essentially, we use positive affirmations to psych ourselves up.

Science (with a capital "S!") hasn't come to agreement on the efficacy of positive affirmations. Some studies say it improves self-esteem and reduces stress levels, while others found that is only the case if you already have high self-esteem (it can have a negative effect for those with a poor self-image).

As with many things in this book, I recommend trying it. If it doesn't work for you, it's not a big deal, and if it does, great. Think of it as expanding your tool kit for self-care—which is never a bad thing.

90

Stepping Away for a Moment

Have so much work to do that you're eating lunch at your desk? While it might seem like the only way to get everything done is by not taking your lunch break, you're actually hurting your productivity.

Our brains weren't meant to run for eight to ten hours straight. Even our cell phones batteries run out if they're consistently used for that long. Think about what your phone is like in low-battery mode: a little dimmer, with less functionality. When we step away from our work, it's like we're recharging our brains. Then, when we return to our desk, we increase the amount we accomplish and reduce the amount of mistakes we make in our work.

The productivity app DeskTime recommends taking a break every fifty-two minutes, for seventeen minutes. If those numbers seem a bit too precise to follow, think about taking a break every hour or so. Take a walk, eat a healthy snack, or talk to a colleague about something besides work.

In the end, your work—and your mental health—will benefit from it.

91
Podcasts

If you're interested in learning more about Zen, and you're looking for something to listen to during your commute, here are a few to get you started:

1. Zencast: Recording podcasts since 2005, mostly from talks held at the Insight Meditation Center in California.
2. Optimal Living Daily: A bit broader, recording on a wide range of topics from fitness to money management.
3. San Francisco Zen Center: A few Zen Centers throughout the country record their talks and make them available as a podcast. The San Francisco Zen Center is one example of what's out there.

92

Time-Tracking Apps

In my group of friends, it can sometimes seem like we're in a competition for who is the busiest. We list our projects, our failed commitments, and bemoan the hours spent in front of a computer instead of with friends and family.

But is it really true?

There's been a movement recently around tracking the time spent on individual projects as well as at work in general. Accordingly, a slew of time-tracking apps have followed. You can use these apps to help you notice how many hours a week you're working (this is especially useful if you work from home), on the commute, and on specific projects that might seem like timesucks.

You might end up realizing that you don't win the "busiest person of the year" award, but you may get some perspective on your life.

93

Seriously: Are You Breathing?

Take a deep breath in through your nose and exhale through your mouth. Repeat two more times (or every chapter until you are really, truly breathing).

94

Brain Games

In an episode of *Sherlock* ("The Abominable Bride"), the delightful Detective Holmes uses the "method of loci" to help solve the crime. Sometimes referred to as the "memory palace" or "mind palace," this technique is said to improve memory and form new neural connections.

To bring this mental workout into the office, create a list of tasks you need to accomplish at work today. Associate each task with an image at a familiar location (or "palace"). For example, if you need to remember to make ten photocopies of a presentation, you can imagine a giant turkey with the presentation instead of feathers, walking around the copy room. Create a different illustration for each item on your to-do list.

This game also works for grocery lists, remembering your bank account number, and recalling important dates.

95
To-Do Lists

I don't know anyone who doesn't get a little endorphin boost any time they cross something off of a to-do list. It's a profound and simple pleasure.

The question is: what do you cross off first? Do you get the most unpleasant item off of the list so the rest of your day can only get better? Do you begin with small, easy successes to energize the rest of the day? Or do you check (pun!) Facebook and Twitter, and then hope everything else flows from there?

If you feel your motivation taking a nose-dive, it might have something to do with the task list you have looming in front of you and how you approach it. Try switching up your order and see if the spark follows.

After Work

Making Time for Friends, Family, and You

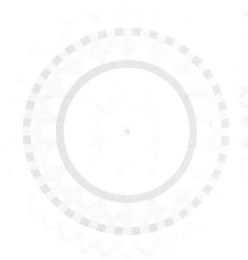

96

Checking Email at Home

When checking email at home (assuming you usually work outside the home), clock into an app that logs your time. At the end of a few weeks, export that time to a spreadsheet. Even before looking at that spreadsheet, write down how many hours you feel comfortable putting in.

Compare that number to the number on the spreadsheet.

If there's a huge disconnect, you now have the record to take to your boss. Even if they don't change your responsibilities, you have solid evidence for when you ask for a raise.

97

Exercise

Some believe that the physical practice of yoga was developed so that our bodies could be strong enough to sit through long periods of mediation. Early texts written about yoga confirm this.

Likewise, many Zen monks exercise to prepare the body for *zazen,* or seated meditation.

While you might not be sitting for hours of mediation, you are probably sitting for hours at a desk. Beyond the hundreds of other reasons to exercise, it can also prepare the body for office Zen.

98

Sleep

We need different amounts of sleep at different stages of our life, and the amount changes based on our gender, genetics, and the activities we engage in during the day.

Whatever the factors, you're still probably not getting enough. Go to bed.

99

Separation of Work and Home

I understand the necessity of checking email from home so that first thing in the morning you're not drowning in a sea of correspondence. If that's part of your work culture, I'm not going to ask you to be a singular force to change that, unless you feel called to.

Here's what you do have the power to do: use time at home to get up to date before the end of the day. Don't constantly update your emails and check your phone—this creates a habit that is absentminded and obsessive. Set aside some time for yourself to work if you need to and do it without guilt. That way, when it isn't *that* time, you're present in *this* moment.

100

Quitting with Compassion

Going out with a bang is always tempting. I once *Office Space*-ed my way out of a particularly toxic work environment. At the moment it felt pretty great, but years later I still think about how I was kind of an asshole (for example, here I am, still writing about it).

Here's a simple rule of thumb: happy people tend not to lash out at other people, happy people don't cause unnecessary drama, and happy people aren't spiteful. If you're quitting because things are terrible, which is often how it goes, quit others as you would want to be quitted. Ten years down the line, you won't still be thinking about how you could have been nicer about it.

101
Retiring

Retire when the work is done.

This is the way of heaven.

—Verse 9, Tao Te Ching (translation by Gia-Fu Feng and Jane English)